Social Media Marketing 2024

By

Robert Hill

Table of Contents

6

Introduction

Social media marketing has emerged as a powerful force in the world of advertising and promotion. In an era dominated by digital technologies and online interactions, businesses, organizations, and individuals have harnessed the potential of social media platforms to reach a vast and diverse audience. This will provide a comprehensive overview of social media marketing, its origins, evolution, significance, and impact on the way we communicate, connect and conduct business in the modern age. Social media marketing refers to the use of various social media platforms, such as Facebook, Instagram, Twitter, LinkedIn, and Pinterest, to promote products, services, or ideas. It involves creating and sharing content with the goal of reaching and engaging a target audience. This can encompass a wide range of activities, from posting text, images, and videos to running paid advertising campaigns on these platforms.

One of the primary reasons social media marketing is crucial is its unparalleled reach and accessibility. Platforms like Facebook and Instagram boast billions of active users, providing businesses with a vast and diverse audience to connect with. This makes it an ideal channel for promoting products or services, building brand awareness, and fostering customer loyalty. Furthermore, social media marketing offers a level of engagement and interaction that traditional marketing methods cannot match. It enables businesses to directly communicate with their audience, receive feedback, and address customer concerns promptly.

This fosters a sense of trust and connection that is invaluable in today's competitive market.

As social media platforms gained popularity and user engagement soared, businesses recognized the potential for reaching their audience in a more direct and personal way. This realization gave birth to the concept of social media marketing. Rather than relying solely on traditional advertising methods, companies began to integrate social media into their marketing strategies. Initially, social media marketing revolved around creating and sharing content organically. Companies established brand profiles on platforms like Facebook, Twitter, and Instagram to engage with their audience, share updates, and respond to customer inquiries. These platforms allowed businesses to showcase their products, services, and values in a more interactive and engaging manner.

Features of social media Profiles provided businesses with tools to manage their online presence effectively. It wasn't long before they recognized the potential for reaching a wider audience by investing in paid social media advertising. Social media platforms began offering advertising solutions, such as promoted posts and sponsored content, enabling businesses to target specific demographics and reach users who might not have discovered them otherwise. The power of social media marketing extends beyond just selling products. It also plays a crucial role in building and maintaining a brand's reputation. Businesses can use social media to establish their brand identity, share their values, and showcase their expertise in their industry. Through consistent and engaging content, they can create a loyal community of followers who become advocates for their brand.

However, social media marketing is not without its challenges. The digital landscape is constantly evolving, and algorithms change frequently. It can be challenging to keep up with the latest trends and ensure that content reaches the intended audience. Moreover, the potential for negative feedback and public relations crises exists, so managing a brand's online reputation is essential. In conclusion, social media marketing is an indispensable tool in today's marketing landscape. Its reach, affordability, interactivity, and data-driven approach make it a key element in any marketing strategy. When executed effectively, social media marketing can boost brand awareness, drive sales, and foster a strong connection with the target audience. Businesses that embrace social media marketing and adapt to its dynamic nature will have a significant advantage in the modern business environment.

You will learn the following concepts from this book, to name a few examples:

- Social Media Marketing: What It Is, How It Works
- How to Become a Social Media Marketer
- How to becomes popular on social media marketing
- How to manage social media
- Social Media Marketing Platforms for 2024
- Advantages and disadvantages of social media marketing

So, Let's Get Started:

Chapter No. 01

Social Media Marketing

Building a company brand, increasing sales, and driving visitors to a website are all goals of social media marketing, which is also known as digital marketing and e-marketing. Social media marketing is the use of social media platforms, which allow users to develop social networks and exchange information. SMM features purpose-built data analytics that enable marketers to measure the performance of their efforts and uncover even more ways to interact with consumers, in addition to providing businesses with a method to communicate with current customers and reach new ones. This is one of the many benefits that SMM offers to businesses.

The explosive rise of interactive digital channels brought social media to levels that compete with even the reach of television and radio in only 18 years, from 2004 (when My Space became the first social media site to achieve one million members) to 2022 (when Facebook became the first social media site to surpass two billion users). At the beginning of the year 2023, there were 4.76 billion people using social media throughout the globe. This represented more than 59% of the total population of the planet. Over eighty percent of customers say that social media, and particularly influencer content, has a significant impact on their purchasing decisions. As a result, marketers in all sectors are driving the evolution of social media marketing (SMM) from a stand-alone tool to a multipronged source of marketing intelligence on an increasingly important and growing audience.

1.1 Components of Social Media Marketing

There are following components of social media marketing

- Strategy
- Planning and Publishing
- Listening and Engagement
- Analytics and Reporting
- Advertising

1.1.1 Strategy

Let's take a moment to stand back and examine the situation from a more macro perspective before you immediately jump in and post anything on social media. The first thing you should do is give some thought to your social media approach. What are some of your objectives? In what ways may using social media help you reach your objectives for your business? Some companies use social media in order to raise their company's brand recognition, while others utilize it in order to increase sales and traffic to their websites. In addition to helping you develop interaction around your brand, building a community, and acting as a customer care channel for your consumers, social media platforms may be of use to you. Which of the several platforms of social media do you want to concentrate on? Facebook, Instagram, Twitter, LinkedIn, Pinterest, and YouTube were named as some of the most prominent significant social media networks. Snapchat was also listed. There are also a number of smaller platforms that are gaining popularity, such as Tumbler, Tik Tok, and Anchor, as well as social messaging services, such as Messenger,

WhatsApp, and WeChat. When you're first getting started, it's preferable to focus on one or two platforms where you believe the majority of your audience is rather than trying to be everywhere.

What kind of information do you want other people to see? What kind of material do you think will be most appealing to your demographic? Are you looking for pictures, videos, or links? Is it material that teaches or is it content that entertains? Developing a marketing persona that represents you and who can guide you through the process of answering these questions is a fantastic place to start. You are free to adjust your approach at any time in response to the success or failure of the posts you make on social media. This need not be a permanent decision.

1.1.2   Planning and Publishing

Having a constant presence on various social media platforms is often the starting point for social media marketing for small companies. The number of individuals who use social media each day is quickly approaching three billion (3,000,000,000!). You are providing a chance for potential clients to become aware of your business by participating in various social media platforms.

Sharing a blog post, a picture, or a video on one of the several social media platforms is all that is required to publish content to social media. It works exactly the same way as if you were sharing on your own personal Facebook page. However, rather of producing and posting material on the spur of the moment, you should instead organize your content ahead of time. In addition, if you want to guarantee that you are making the most of your reach on social media, you need to create fantastic material that is appealing to your audience at the appropriate frequency and time. There is now a wide selection of social media scheduling software available, such as Buffer Publish, which may assist you in automatically publishing your material at the time of day that you want. This not only saves you time but also enables you to communicate with your audience at the precise moment in which they are most likely to interact with the material you provide.

1.1.3 Listening and Engagement

Conversations about your brand will rise as both your company and the number of people following you on social media expand. People will either contact you directly, comment on your social media posts, or tag you in their own social media posts. People will also tag you in their own social media posts. There's also a possibility that people may discuss your business on social media without informing you about it. As a result, you should listen to what people are saying about your company on social media. You have the opportunity to surprise and pleasure the person if it is a statement that is favourable. In every other case, you have the ability to provide help and make adjustments before a problem becomes more severe.

You have the option to manually check all of your alerts across all of the social media platforms; however, this method is inefficient, and it will not allow you to see postings that were not tagged with your company's social media profile. You might, instead, make use of a social media listening and engagement tool that compiles all of your social media mentions and messages, even those that did not tag your company's social media profile in the post in question.

1.1.4 Analytics and Reporting

You will want to keep track of how well your social media marketing is doing along the road, regardless of whether you are posting content or participating in conversations on social media. Are you reaching a larger audience on social media compared to the previous month? How many compliments are sent your way each month on average? How many individuals have used the hashtag associated with your brand while posting on social media?

The social media platforms, in and of themselves, provide some of this information at a fundamental level. You may utilize one of the many social media analytics tools that are now accessible, such as Buffer Analyse, to get more in-depth analytics information or to simply compare results across other social media platforms.

1.1.5 Advertising

Advertising on social media platforms is one avenue that you may want to investigate if you have more money available to invest in expanding your social media marketing efforts. Through the use of social media advertisements, you are able to communicate with a larger audience than just the people that are following you.

These days, advertising platforms for social media are so strong that you may be quite selective about the people to whom your adverts are shown. You are able to construct target audiences by basing them on a variety of factors, including their demographics, interests, behaviours, and more. When you have many social media advertising campaigns running at the same time, you may want to think about utilizing a social media advertising platform so that you can make adjustments in bulk, automate procedures, and better optimize your advertisements.

1.2 Why Is Social Media Marketing is So Powerful?

The unmatched capabilities of social media in three fundamental aspects of marketing—connection, engagement, and consumer data—are the source of the effectiveness of social media marketing.

Connection: Not only does social media make it possible for companies to connect with their customers in ways that were not possible in the past, but it also provides an extraordinary variety of channels through which companies can connect with their target audiences. These channels include content platforms (like YouTube) and social sites (like Facebook) as well as microblogging services (like X platform).

Engagement: The ever-changing nature of engagement on social media, whether it takes the form of active conversation or passive "liking," allows companies to take advantage of free advertising possibilities generated by eWOM (electronic word-of-mouth) recommendations made by both current and prospective clients. Not only is the positive contagion effect that comes from eWOM a key motivator of consumer choices, but the fact that these interactions take place on the social network makes them quantifiable as well. For instance, companies are able to assess their social equity, which is another name for the return on investment (ROI) generated by their various social media marketing activities.

Customer Data: A social media marketing strategy that is adequately developed will provide another useful resource that can be used to increase marketing results. This resource is customer data. SMM technologies have the potential to not only harvest consumer data but also to transform this gold into practical market analysis — or even to utilize the data to crowd source new strategies — so that businesses are not overwhelmed by the 3Vs of big data, which are volume, variety, and velocity. This allows businesses to avoid being stymied by the big data phenomenon.

1.3   How Social Media Marketing Works

When social media platforms like Facebook and Instagram took off, it not only changed the way we connect with one another but also the way businesses are able to influence the consumer behaviour of their customers. This includes everything from the promotion of content that drives engagement to the extraction of geographic, demographic, and personal information that makes messaging resonate with users.

1.3.1   Action Plan

Your social media marketing plan will be more successful if it is more narrowly focused. In order to construct a social media marketing campaign that includes both an execution framework and success indicators, the industry-leading software supplier Hootsuite, which specializes in social media management, suggests the following action plan

- Align the aims of SMM with the explicit business objectives

19

- Become knowledgeable about your ideal clientele in terms of their age, location, income, job title, industry and hobbies.
- Carry out a competitive examination of your rivals, examining both their triumphs and their setbacks.
- Perform an audit of your present SMM, focusing on both accomplishments and problems.
- Develop a schedule for the dissemination of SMM material
- Produce material that is the finest of its kind.
- Monitor results and make necessary adjustments to the SMM strategy

1.3.2 Customer Relationship Management

When compared to conventional marketing, social media marketing has a number of unique benefits. One of these advantages is the fact that SMM includes two forms of contact that allow focused customer relationship management (CRM) solutions. These kinds of interaction include customer-to-customer and firm-to-customer communication. SMM may measure customer value both directly (via purchases) and indirectly (through product recommendations), but conventional marketing can only track customer value by collecting buy activity. In other words, traditional marketing is limited to tracking customer value.

1.3.3 Shareable Content

Sticky content is a marketing word for beautiful material that hooks consumers at first sight, convinces them to acquire things, and then makes them want to share the content with their friends and family. Businesses may also turn the increased interconnection that is provided by SMM into the development of sticky content. This kind of word-of-mouth advertising not only reaches an audience that would otherwise be unreachable, but it also carries the implicit endorsement of someone the receiver knows and trusts. As a result, the development of content that is easily shared is one of the most essential ways that social media marketing promotes growth.

1.3.4 Earned Media

Social media marketing is also the most effective technique for a firm to enjoy the advantages of another kind of earned media, which is a phrase for brand exposure via any source other than paid advertising. This type of earned media consists of customer-created product evaluations and recommendations.

1.3.5 Viral Marketing

Viral marketing is another method for social media marketing (SMM) that depends on the audience to produce the message. It is a sales tactic that seeks to spark the fast spread of product information via word-of-mouth communication. It is deemed viral when a marketing message gets shared with the general public much beyond the population that it was initially targeted towards. This is a very easy and affordable technique to drive sales of a product or service.5

1.3.6 Customer Segmentation

Companies are able to guarantee that their marketing efforts are focused on their particular target audiences by using social media marketing (SMM), since consumer segmentation on SMM is far more detailed than on conventional marketing channels.

1.3.7 Tracking Metrics

According to Sprout Social, the most important social media marketing metrics to track are customer-centric. These metrics include engagement (likes, comments, shares, and clicks); impressions (how many times a post shows up); reach/virility (how many unique views an SMM post has); share of voice (how far a brand reaches in the online sphere); referrals (how a user lands on a site); and conversions (when a user makes a purchase on a site). However, there is still another extremely essential measure that focuses on the company itself, and that is the response rate and time (the frequency with which the company replies to consumer messages and the speed with which it does so).

Always follow the guideline of aligning each business objective with a meaningful statistic when attempting to establish which metrics to monitor amid the sea of data that is generated by social media for a company that is trying to figure out which metrics to track. Use a social media analytics tool that monitors the efficacy of your campaign in relation to a certain target if one of your company's goals is to increase conversions resulting from a social media marketing (SMM) campaign by 15% in the span of three months.

1.4   Pros and Cons of Social Media Marketing

1.4.1   Pros of Social Media Marketing

A new set of advantages has arisen as a direct result of the proliferation of marketing via social media. Platforms for social media offer an effective medium for reaching and connecting with a broad audience, which may contribute to increased brand exposure and recognition.

Building closer ties with consumers and fostering customer loyalty may be aided by engaging with them via various social media outlets. Because it is often a more cost-effective alternative when compared to more conventional ways of promotion, it is more enticing for establishments that are just beginning their marketing efforts. The very nature of social media marketing offers a multitude of advantages as well. By posting links to your website or blog on social media, you may assist improve the amount of traffic that visits your site and the possibility that visitors will make a purchase. In addition, social media platforms provide a method for collecting feedback from clients in real time, enabling quick contact and making it easier to communicate with one another.

Another advantage of marketing on social media is that it may be both general and specific at the same time. Shares, likes, comments, and other types of interaction may help companies gain a bigger audience on social media, which can also boost their level of engagement with their customers. This is particularly true when taking into consideration the instances in which consumers transmit information to those who are not clients. On the other hand, social media platforms provide users with a variety of targeting options, which enables businesses to zero in on certain demographics, interests, and behaviours of their target audiences and then send personalized content to those people.

1.4.2 Cons of Social Media Marketing
The use of social media for marketing purposes comes with a number of advantages, but it also has a number of disadvantages and complexities. It takes time and work to

have a good social media presence, and company owners frequently need to participate in constant content creation and conversation on a regular basis. A strong awareness of the different social media platforms, together with the skills to generate interesting content, analyse data, and make choices based on the findings of such analyses, are required for effective social media marketing. Each platform usually demands a specialized expertise and calls for one of its own. In addition, social media sites often update both their algorithms and their regulations, making it more difficult to forecast future success and to sustain existing levels of success.

Even if social media makes it simple to engage with consumers, it also gives those customers a forum to publicly air their complaints and concerns about a company's products or services. It is possible that this will have the unintended result of establishing a public forum, which, if not managed correctly, may be harmful to the image of a corporation. Last but not least, it may be challenging to have a good grasp on the return on investment for social media marketing. Measuring the efficiency and return on investment of social media marketing may be difficult since it often entails monitoring several measures, analyzing complicated data sets, and making assumptions about why customers may have responded in a variety of ways.

Chapter No. 02

How to Become a Social Media Marketer

As a social media marketer, it will be your job to promote the goods and services offered by your firm across a variety of online venues. You'll also make use of consumer data in order to communicate with, influence, and interact with customers. Doesn't it seem straightforward enough? But how do you begin in the first place? Although you could find this question daunting, the reality is that you might be more prepared for it than you realize. After all, you've been cultivating a following on your own social media platforms while also selling your own brand. You will be able to complete your skill set in media marketing with the help of a few helpful hints.

2.1   Developing Basic Skills

Pay attention to the three most important social media networks. Although it may seem to be the reverse, it is preferable to specialize in one or two unique platforms rather than generalize over a large number of various ones. Facebook, Twitter, and LinkedIn are now the three most significant social media sites for advertising. Because social media platforms undergo regular updates, marketing strategies that were formerly successful are becoming less relevant as a result. Maintaining an active presence across several platforms will be a far more challenging task than concentrating on just one or two.

- Maintain an up-to-date knowledge base by either subscribing to marketing blogs for media platforms or registering for platform newsletters, such as Facebook's Marketing Partner Weekly Update.

- Investigate available internet resources in order to educate yourself on various marketing strategies applicable to the platform(s) of your choice. On their own YouTube channels or Facebook pages, a lot of experts in social media marketing provide helpful tips.
- What works and what doesn't work depends on the business you're in, the platform you use, and the audience you're trying to reach. It is essential to do ongoing research and development on a variety of post formats in order to maintain a competitive advantage.

2.1.1   Research your customer base

Adapting a marketing strategy to a certain industry will need some creativity. You will first need to decide which industry you will work in as a marketer, such as the fashion business, the automobile sector, or the technology industry. Pick one in which you have both an interest and a passion in order to be able to impart information while maintaining your own enthusiasm in the topic. Examine the discussion boards that may be found on the websites of the leading companies in your sector. What is everyone talking about these days? Learn more about your consumer base by listening in on these discussions.

- In order to find and keep track of subjects that are important to your client base, you should create a Reddit account and subscribe to subreddits in your business.
- There's no reason why doing research should be dull! Create a list of subject areas in your industry using color-coded spreadsheets by using Google Spreadsheets

or Excel and making use of the Colour coding feature. You may boost the diversity of your postings by using this list.

2.1.2 Observe the marketing strategies of successful companies

Follow a few firms whose work you appreciate, and then follow those companies on the media platform(s) of your choice. Observe and make notes on their advertising strategies. Pose the question to yourself, "How might I recreate this? What would I do differently if I could do it over? What might I do with this to market a product that I am selling? Do not be afraid to question yourself; having conversations with oneself is very natural.

- Create a bookmark or take a snapshot of the advertising campaigns of the firms that you follow that are your favourite. Consider drawing ideas for your own advertisement from these examples.
- Install an RSS reader on your computer so that you can keep up with the latest advertising-related news from publications and websites such as AdAge, PSFK, Creativity Magazine, and eMarketer.

2.1.3 Train yourself to post and update regularly

Even if it's only your status on Facebook, you should get in the habit of updating it often. Even if you're feeling exhausted, you have to keep going until you win and keep a continuous stream of postings coming in. Keep fighting through it! When you put in more effort and practice, things will become easier. If your readers believe that you are bombarding them with pointless marketing via spam, they will most likely unfollow you or ban you from their feeds.

Make sure your posts are still relevant and helpful. It is important to steer clear of repetition if you want your writing to seem original and engaging.

2.1.4   Intern or volunteer to build experience

To get work experience, you may gain it via interning or volunteering. You will get knowledge of various marketing strategies from seasoned professionals by shadowing them in their daily work as a volunteer or intern, which is analogous to the work of a secret agent. Secret agent, make a mental note of the strategies that worked and the ones that were a horrible failure. Avoid wasting time in your own marketing efforts by steering clear of strategies that seem appealing on paper but are ineffective in practice.

- Make contact with a local charity, politician, school, or company and convey your desire to assist that organization's social media marketing department in exchange for volunteer hours.
- To increase your visibility and reputation in your chosen business, you should write a personal blog that covers themes related to that area. Gain some writing experience by contributing to a blog that is updated on a weekly basis for a local company.

2.2   Building a Professional Network

Join several social groups related to your field. Meetup and Sprout Social are two examples of social networking sites that might bring you in contact with people who have an interest in the field in which you will be promoting your products or services. Establish connections with the aforementioned individuals. Share with them the ways in which you can assist them, and vice versa. They might prove to be quite important in the future.

- Let folks in your chosen field know about some of the recent projects you've worked on, as well as the ones you're looking forward to working on in the future. This is a sly method of signaling to other people certain areas in which you excel and in which they may be interested.
- Conduct an internet search to locate professional gatherings, expos, and organizations such as the New York Social Media Club and the New Media Expo. Participate in these activities and be sure to share contact information with the other people there.

2.2.1   Cultivate your online presence

Develop your presence in the internet world. Participate in discussions that are relevant to your field on social media platforms like Facebook, Twitter, and Instagram. Build up your own following on both Twitter and Facebook. Get your social media account featured on news websites that are read by millions of people by enlisting the assistance of press release companies. If you have a significant number of followers, prospective employers will be more interested in speaking with you.

- To increase the level of community involvement on your Facebook page, share posts that are relevant to your sector that are published by other organizations or innovative research.
- If you want to connect with influential people in your field on Twitter, you may do so by tweeting directly to those individuals by using the sign followed by the user's name. On Facebook, you may do the same thing by connecting other users' postings to your own.
- To get the attention of other internet users, you should reply to the postings they make. Do not be scared to take a stand or speak your opinion on topics in a courteous manner; do not be frightened to do either.

2.2.2   Develop meaningful relationship

Establish significant connections with others who are also in marketing. It seems like you have a busy week ahead. It may be challenging to find the time to nurture and maintain important work connections. Why not run over your customer list for one hour once a week? You could schedule that time apart.

- Use the phone to get in touch with your contacts. In order to keep the discussion brief while yet making it personal, you may say something along the lines of "I'm a little busy today, but I wanted to call and see how you were doing."
- Connecting with contacts via email is analogous to having talks over the phone. Make the message seem more natural by using a basic template and adding a few of your own unique remarks to it

2.2.3 Collaborate with other social media marketers

Collaborate with other people who are marketing on social media. Creating a successful career for yourself in marketing might be demanding, but there is an old proverb that says "Many hands make for light labour." After establishing professional relationships, reach out to other media marketers and propose collaborating on a personal project, such as marketing for an event or professional organization you are associated with.

- If there are aspects of your social media marketing abilities that need improvement, consider working with a partner who excels in those areas in which you struggle.
- If you want to connect with other people, you may say something like, "I've got Twitter under control, but I think managing that along with Facebook would be overwhelming." What do you say we combine our efforts, and you take charge of Facebook?
- Your project will have enhanced engagement from the online followings of other contributors, which is an extra plus (and who doesn't love bonuses?). Who doesn't love bonuses?

2.3 Landing a Job

Gather evidence in the form of facts and testimonials to demonstrate your abilities. Tracking your media interaction may be done with the use of analytic tools such as Google Analytics, Data hero, or Yahoo Web Analytics. Utilize the platform's analytic capabilities, such as the "Insights" option that can be found on Facebook company pages.

31

- Pay close attention to the ways in which you positively affected the growth, savings, and time of the organization. Utilize a spreadsheet to record and monitor your metrics.
- Employers place a great value on measurable evidence that demonstrates your talents. Saying something like, "I was able to increase unique views by 250% in three months," for example, is more effective than making general claims.
- When applying for jobs with different firms, it is important to be truthful. It is possible that you may be requested to back up your data. If you are unable to because you have manipulated the figures, it may be detrimental to your reputation.

2.3.1 Put together a portfolio

Create a portfolio of your work. Gather together some examples of your very finest work. Create a table of contents for these examples, and then immediately after that, compose a brief introduction in which you discuss yourself, your objectives, and the samples that are included. Showcase the breadth of your abilities by providing examples drawn from a variety of projects.

- Some of the most valuable examples of work to add in a portfolio are things like integrated marketing efforts, novel concepts, and highly successful campaigns.
- A digital portfolio may be published to a professional website or a platform page, such as LinkedIn or Facebook. Both of these options are available to you.
- Bringing a printed copy of your portfolio to interviews is a great way to demonstrate that you are well prepared. The contents should be printed on high-

quality paper and then placed in a binder that was purchased specifically for that purpose.

2.3.2 Protect your online image

Guard your reputation on the internet. When it comes to guarding your reputation on the internet, the old adage "loose lips sink ships" rings particularly true. If you mistakenly post anything unsuitable or do so while under the influence of strong emotions, you risk losing followers and damaging your reputation in the online community. Before making any posts public, give them great consideration. Before you publish your content online, you should run it past a trusted friend, colleague, or supervisor to ensure that it does not include any offensive material that you could inadvertently share.

- When you begin to feel emotional, allow yourself some time to settle down before doing anything else. Give yourself a day or two to mull about a post if you're ever on the fence about whether or not to respond to it.
- Maintaining a consistent appearance is one of the most critical factors in controlling your image. If you submit or publish questionable material inconsistently, you may come seem as untrustworthy to your audience.

2.3.3 Write a unique resume

Create a one-of-a-kind CV for yourself. When you apply for a job, you are, in essence, promoting yourself, right? Therefore, you should put your best foot forward by composing a one-of-a-kind and intelligent resume. Put your design abilities on display with one or two straightforward and relevant graphics. Include links to the social media profiles you maintain for both your personal and business lives. Demonstrate that you understand what customers want and how to market it effectively. Using visually appealing methods to promote goods and services, such as photographs and memes, is an effective approach to grab people's attention. Evidence of your ability to incorporate visual aspects into your work will be something that potential employers want to see.

Chapter No. 03

How to Become Popular on Social Media

Maybe you want to become popular on social media to make money, or maybe you simply want to share your art and ideas with others. No matter the reason, there are some steps you can take to increase your social media following and gain popularity. Develop a routine for posting your unique content, and interact with followers to increase your online presence. Commit to your new endeavor—it may take a little while to become popular, but you can do it!

3.1 Choosing a Platform

Choose one platform to focus your attention on. You can definitely use multiple social media platforms, but choose one to start with. Trying to master too many platforms at once will weaken your social media presence, which isn't what you want. Go ahead and reserve your username on multiple platforms, but wait to start developing them until you've spent time becoming proficient in your first choice. Once you feel you can easily handle the platform and are regularly posting new content, incorporate an additional platform. If you use too many social media platforms, it'll be impossible to keep up with comments and questions. Start small, and then increase your platforms as you gain more experience.

3.1.1 Use Instagram or a blog

Use Instagram or a blog to focus on lifestyle and image-centered information. Writing, cooking, beauty, and fitness interests do well on these platforms because they're primarily image- and information-based. Instagram is great for fast-paced content creation, whereas a blog will allow you to dive a little more deeply into different topics.

Instagram can also be a great tool to use to connect with other creators like yourself very quickly. It's easy to use hashtags to search for relatable content, and people check their accounts often, which means you will have more foot traffic than you might initially get on a blog.

3.1.2 Fast paced medium

Choose a fast-paced medium to showcase your humor and wit. Sites like Twitter and Reddit are constantly updating. People scroll through content quickly, pausing for mere seconds to check out a post. You can also get help from press release agencies to help get your profile on news sites that millions of people read about. These are great places to interact with others about politics, pop culture, and comedy. Twitter is used a lot for news, sports, and popular media; Reddit includes forums and deep-dives into almost any topic you can think of. Twitter and Reddit also let you post photos and interact with others easily by "liking," retweeting, reposting, and commenting on content quickly.

3.1.3 Pick Facebook to promote your presence

Pick Facebook to promote your presence to a lot of people. In addition to sharing content with all the people you're friends with, you can also promote posts (for a fee) and reach people who aren't on your friends list. It's also a great platform to connect with businesses in your community, as most companies have Facebook pages. Facebook also provides a lot of helpful statistics about your posts and content, showing you how many people click on your posts and engage with them, what times of the day are busiest, and what demographic is interested in your content.

3.1.4 Use videos and podcast to explain something

If you're an expert in baking, history, politics, exercise, or tutorials of some sort, creating a YouTube channel, blog, or podcast on Sound Cloud or iTunes would be a great way to start sharing your information. This gives you a little more space to go into detail and could be a great resource for followers to learn something new. This is a great way to start exposing yourself to more followers. A lot of people would rather watch (or listen) than read something, so creating a dynamic video or podcast is a cool way to show your personality and reach more people.

3.1.5 How to cross-post your content

While you could create new material for each platform, you could also link your accounts so that they're always updated with the same new material (or at least a link to the new material). For example, if you primarily blog and use Instagram, you'll probably post a lot more photos to Instagram than new entries on your blog, which is totally fine. But when you do post a new blog, make an announcement on your Instagram post so your followers know there is new material. As you're starting out, try to keep things simple—learn to master a platform and post good content, and once you're doing these things, you'll have a good base on which you can build your brand.

3.2 Posting New Content

Choose a theme for your content, like beauty or education. Choose something you're passionate and knowledgeable about. Maybe it's something like comedy, cooking, makeup techniques, shopping, singing, fashion, or impressions. The best way to keep yourself and others interested in your content is to be passionate about it yourself.

- Resist the temptation to copy other popular online presences. They're famous because of their unique views and interests, and you can be, too. It's okay to gain inspiration from someone else—just make sure to recreate that content you love so that it is uniquely yours.
- Settling on a niche to focus on is really important— finding a niche that works for you will help you stand out from the crowd.

3.2.1 Create new content

Choose one day per week that is dedicated to content creation. If you're in school, maybe one afternoon is dedicated to this. Or if you have a family, maybe Sunday mornings when everyone is sleeping in is a good time for you. Write it down in your calendar and commit to it.

- Use this time to create all of your content for the upcoming week. You won't post everything you create that day at once, but it'll be ready to go throughout the week.
- This time slot will guarantee that you have new content to post. Work on blogs, photo editing, links, videos, tutorials, and whatever else you're creating.
- Be prepared to invest months and months of time before your following starts to grow. Some of the most popular

social media presences have been around and working on their content for years.

3.2.2 Proofreading or viewing your work to correct errors

From grammatical errors to misreporting facts, spend about ten minutes reviewing your content before you send it out into the world. Think about how the post is going to appear to your followers will the wording or content make sense? Is the message on brand? Is it free of major mistakes? Especially if you're doing any kind of social commentary or reporting, it's important to double-check names, dates, and facts so that you remain a trustworthy online presence.

3.2.3 Keep your followers engaged

Even if you schedule out your main posts and have a few things you do every week, try to engage with your audience and post something almost every day, even if it's something small like a selfie outside your favorite coffee shop or a quote from a book you're reading. If you miss a day or two here and there, that is totally okay! It can also be helpful for your mental health to take a break from social media every once in a while, too.

3.2.4 Schedule your posts

Schedule your posts to appear during high-traffic times of day. From Monday through Friday, Instagram is busiest from 12 pm to 1 pm, Facebook is best hit between 12 pm and 3 pm during the work week, and Twitter has the highest traffic around 3 pm. Think about the times you're most likely to check your accounts, like during midday breaks and the late evening hours. Avoid posting early in the morning. Most people are busy getting ready for work or are invested in their tasks for the day.

3.2.5 Vary your content to keep it engaging

Rather than just posting how-to videos, if you're a beauty blogger, for example, try also posting some reviews of new products or interviews with other fashion and beauty bloggers. Fun facts, inspiration, memes, contests, throwbacks, FAQ sessions, polls, tours, and travel content can all work toward keeping your content fresh and exciting. Try tracking what kind of content you post for one month, and then look at what areas you could expand upon to diversify your posts.

3.3 Gaining Followers

Use hashtags to help new followers find your content. Pay attention to the hashtags that other personalities use. For example, if you have a bookstagram (an Instagram that features photos of books and reviews), you'll notice bookstagram, #bookworm, #bibliophile, amreading, and shelfiesunday. For any given category, you can search online for the most popular hashtags to end your post with.

Sites like Instagram will also make hashtag suggestions once you start typing, and they will show you how many other posts are using that hashtag. The higher the number, the more likely someone will find your post when they search that tag. Use specific hashtags that are tailored to your content rather than super popular, vague ones like #beauty or #fashion. It will be easier for people to find you that way.

3.3.1 be genuine

Be genuine to draw in more followers. Followers can tell if you're being fake or pretending to be interested in something. That's why it's important to post content that you're truly interested in. And the great thing about the internet is that there is space for everybody, from Star Wars fanatics to beauty experts. Be true to yourself! Don't forget that what your peers in real life think is cool might be really different from what people online think. The best way to find online popularity is to start by being yourself.

3.3.2 Interact with followers and ask questions to boost your social media presence

Interact with followers and ask questions to boost your social media presence. Avoid just posting content without checking back on any responses. Spend 15-30 minutes per day looking back at notifications and responding to people's questions or comments. Also, don't be afraid to ask questions of your followers to get them talking or simply to learn something new. For example, if you make a post about a new recipe, you could ask, "What are some of your favorite cookie baking tips, readers? I'd love to know!"

3.3.3 Follow people who have similar content

This works on two levels: you will be inspired by their content and hopefully will create more new material, and people who follow them will be more likely to find your content, too, because of your shared interests. Remember to not copy or plagiarize anyone else's content. You can let it inspire you to create something new, but copying it outright is a form of intellectual property theft.

3.3.4   Network

Network in real life to make connections and grow your following. Your online presence is important, but meeting new people at events is another great way to get inspiration and become a bigger personality online. Attend events that pertain to your interests—if you're a baker, take some cooking classes; if you're a musician, attend open mic events; if you're a fashion blogger, go to fashion shows. You could even create business cards that have your social media handles on them so you can hand them out to new contacts.

3.3.5   Consider paying to promote your content

A lot of sites will allow you to advertise your posts to a targeted demographic for a really small amount of money. For example, Facebook lets your promote posts to hundreds of people for as little as $5. Instagram provides a similar feature. If this is something you're interested in, check out your social media sites to find out what options are available to you. You definitely don't have to pay money to become popular on social media, but it can help you reach a wider audience.

3.4   Keeping Your Brand Consistent

Use the same username across all social media platforms if you can. This makes it easy for followers to find you. This is also a good way to make sure no one else gets a hold of your great name! If you can't use the same username across all platforms, try to make them as similar as possible.

3.4.1   Create a consistent schedule for posting

Rather than taking your social media popularity day-by-day, plan ahead for success. Set time on your calendar to create and post new content. For example, let's say you have a baking blog—on Mondays you could always post a new recipe, on Wednesdays you could do a giveaway, and on Saturdays you could do a live feed. Decide what kind of content you want to be sharing, and find a repeatable way to work.

You can research lots of different popular bloggers and social media persons who share how they create and manage new content. A lot of them plan out their posts several weeks to a month in advance.

3.4.2   Automate your posts and manage all your accounts

There are quite a few apps out there (some of which are free and some which aren't) that will let you manage all your accounts and set a posting schedule from one place. This saves you time and ensures that your new content is being posted consistently. It also frees up some of your time so you can focus on interacting with followers. Hootsuite, Buffer, Sprout Social, Agorapulse, Sendible, and Social Pilot are all popular management tools. Look at the abilities and reviews for each one to find the best one for your content.

3.4.3   Remember what your theme

Chances are, your followers are like-minded people. If you switch what your message is all about, you'll disorient them and probably lose followers. For example, if you have a movie-reviewing blog, people might not be as interested in reading about fashion tips. It's okay to be interested in multiple things and to show your varied interests, but try to keep the main thing the main thing.

Chapter No. 04

How to manage Social Media Marketing

Your life must be quite busy as you are in charge of the social media accounts. You are under a lot of time pressure, but in addition to developing efficient tactics and managing various social media accounts, you also need to be on top of exploring new prospects for marketing growth and reporting on your success. And as if all of this weren't difficult enough already, your social media teams are expanding. This indicates that you need strong management skills in order to construct effective processes and produce outcomes. We are aware that things may seem overwhelming at times. Because of this, we felt the need to produce a step-by-step tutorial that explains how to handle social media in a more effective manner, including topics such as persona analysis, content generation, and listening.

4.1   What is social media marketing management?

The full power of managing a company's social media marketing presence extends much beyond the domain of pre-scheduling postings, which is only one aspect of this. It's about getting people talking about things that matter, making real relationships with other people, and building a thriving community around your business. You may turn interested bystanders into enthusiastic advocates by optimizing your methods for bottom-of-the-funnel conversions. This will not only drive increased engagement rates, but it will also unleash the untapped potential for company development.

The process of analyzing audiences on social media and developing a strategy that is specific to those audiences, developing and distributing content for social media profiles, monitoring online conversations, collaborating with influencers, providing community service, and monitoring, measuring, and reporting on social media performance and return on investment are all components of the social media management process. All of these activities, which were formerly relegated to the background by businesses, are now front and center in the marketing tactics used by those enterprises. Because the social media platforms provide excellent potential to make money — provided, of course, that you handle your social channels in a manner that is well-organized and productive.

4.2 Why is an efficient social media management process important?

It is difficult to overstate the commercial possibilities of social networks. Utilizing social media platforms to effectively drive business goals throughout the marketing funnel, such as boosting shop visits and brand recognition, is possible for brands because to the versatility of these platforms. In point of fact, 43% of company owners make all of their judgments based on information derived from social media.

However, in order for them to be successful in this endeavour, they need social media teams that are effective. When it comes to social media marketing, the number of individuals you need to commit to this tactic is directly proportional to the number of objectives you have set for yourself. Because of this need, social media teams will ultimately need to adopt more sophisticated organizational structures. If you have a huge brand, you may even have many teams located in various locations and parts of the globe, each using a unique strategy in order to achieve the specific goals they have set for themselves. How can we ensure that all of these individuals collaborate closely with one another to get the most possible benefit from social media?

4.3   How can I get started with managing my social media accounts?

Don't worry about not knowing how to begin optimizing the way you handle social media if you don't know how to start. It's something that has a lot of marketers scratching their heads. In order to get off to a good start, there are three essential things that you need to make sure you do:

- Carry out a review of your social media accounts.
- Make a choice about the appropriate social media channels.
- Conduct research on your ideal customers.

Since doing so will provide you with crucial information that will point your efforts in social media marketing in the appropriate direction, and since you can only get this information by performing the tasks. As a consequence of this, you will be able to focus your resources on initiatives that are successful and reduce your investment in those that are not.

4.3.1   Conducting a social media audit

An assessment of your social media accounts may almost always make your social media management better:

- It will provide you with a detailed representation of how well your approach is being implemented.
- It will enable you to identify the areas in which you are squandering your resources.
- It will demonstrate which social channels are producing the greatest number of results.
- It will illustrate the influence that social media has on the outcomes of your website

How exactly do you go about doing a health check on your social media accounts?

- **First,** compile a list of all of the social media accounts associated with your firm. This should include profiles from various countries as well as those associated with your various sub-brands.
- **Step 2:** Use social media analytics to review your key performance metrics, such as the growth of your followers, engagement (including the average engagement rates for particular months), publishing frequency, most engaging content formats, top-performing posts, traffic sources, community sentiment, question response rate, average response time, audience interests, demographics, and behaviours. Step 3: Implement any changes that you find necessary based on the results of step 2 and any other relevant findings.
- **Step 3:** Conduct an in-depth analysis of the collected data to pinpoint specific problem areas. If you see a decrease in the level of interaction with your material, for instance, this might be the consequence of poor content quality, imprecise targeting, or an inappropriate publication frequency.

That is precisely the kind of information you need in order to identify flaws in your plan. From that vantage point, you will be able to take the first steps towards resolving them and making your operations related to social media management more effective.

4.3.2   Decide on the right social media platforms

Selecting the appropriate platform is an additional essential step towards achieving more effective management of social media. Following an analysis of your brand's use of social media, you may find that some channels are ineffective in promoting your business overall. If this is the case, you should make it a priority to investigate how much work will be required to get the outcomes you want. A great deal also relies on the location of your audience. If you find out during your study, for example, that the majority of your audience is on Twitter, but your presence on the platform is not even close to being strong, then it is clear that you need to work on making improvements. If the results you've gotten haven't been that impressive and your target demographic can be found elsewhere, you might think about moving your resources to a new channel. However, before you go ahead and accomplish so, you should first ask yourself the following questions:

- What are the goals I have set for my company (such as increasing brand recognition, the number of leads generated, website traffic, and conversions, etc.)? Will I be able to achieve the goals I have set for my company using this platform? How much money will I need to invest in order to achieve my objectives?
- Will I be able to operate the platform with an efficiency that will allow me to achieve a favourable return on

investment? Will the sum be sufficient to warrant the investment required for marketing on the platform?

- What are the demographics of the community that is present on the platform, and do they align with the demographics of the audience that I want to reach?
- Does the platform have an audience that matches my target demographic that is both present and active? Will I be able to communicate with them successfully?
- How well-known is the platform among marketing professionals? How much unique material will I need to develop in order to differentiate myself?
- Is there anybody who directly competes with me on this platform? How are things going with them? Will I be able to do better than they do?

4.3.3   Analyze your target audience

When it comes to effective management of social media, understanding your community on such platforms is the most important factor. Analyzing your followers may have a number of beneficial effects, such as strengthening your connections with existing customers, producing material that is more relevant to your audience's interests, and increasing the number of conversions you get via social media.

If you do not do market research in advance, you run the chance of going in the incorrect direction, which will result in the loss of both money and other resources. To get started, divide your audience into several personas based on the attributes they all have in common; you can accomplish this by utilizing this customer persona template that is completely free. You may also allow artificial intelligence perform the work for you if you want your life to be simpler. There's a good chance that different types of customers will make up your identities. For instance, you may have a group of teenagers who are interested in sports and another group of adults who are in their 30s reading the Facebook page for Digiday and interacting with the information there. If you have this knowledge, you will be able to make more efficient use of your resources and put more of your attention on the activities that are most successful within your community.

4.4 Stock up on the right social media management tools

Tools for advanced social media management are an absolute must when it comes to successfully developing, implementing, and assessing your social media marketing plan.

4.4.1 Top- to middle-of-the-funnel tools

Tools for the upper and intermediate portions of the sales funnel. It is very vital to do research on your audience at the top and middle of your sales funnel. People who are still in these phases are considered to be prospective clients even if they are frequently referred to as an unknown audience. The more you are able to learn about these consumers, the more successfully you will be able to nurture them towards conversion via individualized marketing strategies. Analytics that are native to social media. The following items are included in the very comprehensive audience data that may be obtained from social media platforms:

- Insights into the demographics, page likes, locations, and activities of your Facebook audience

- Insights from Instagram, including the top places, hours, and days of the week when your followers are most active
- Analytical tools for Twitter, including information on demographics, lifestyle, consumer behaviour, and mobile footprint
- Analyses of LinkedIn users' demographics, job functions, seniority levels, industries, firm sizes, and employment situations

The Audience Analytics feature of Facebook enables you to see your audience segmented into personas according to the demographics, interests, and behaviours that they exhibit. As a direct consequence of this, you won't need to devote as much effort to doing audience research manually.

4.5   Content management tools

The process of managing social media includes a number of steps, one of which is content production, which is an essential but also very difficult one. Test out one or more of these tools to expedite and improve the organization of your content workflow:

Tools for generating content ideas

- Keeping an eye on social media to find out what themes are currently popular online and how you can capitalize on them
- Analytics for social media, so you can keep track of what your rivals are publishing and draw inspiration from some of the strategies that have worked best for them.
- Conducting research on your target demographic in order to comprehend the kind of material to which they favourable react

- Content management tools, which allow you to locate hot articles online and repost them, as well as hundreds of top social media posts that will resonate with each of your audience personas;

Tools for the development of content

- Unsplash, Pexels, and Stocksnap are three websites you may visit to get free stock photos of a high standard.
- Canva, BeFunky, and Adobe Express allow you to create stunning graphics for your social media postings.
- Create entertaining social films that your fans will want to share by using Filmore, Lumen5, or Capcut.
- Google Docs, Confluence, and Nuclino are all excellent platforms on which you and your team can work together to draught social media text.

Calendars for publishing content on social media

- Google Calendar — Use the graphical calendar that Google provides to conveniently schedule your postings.
- Using a spreadsheet from Google, you may make your own editorial schedule that is specific to your requirements.
- Free calendar templates; save time with pre-made versions of popular social network calendars
- material calendar planner – get a visual overview of your social media material, schedule and evaluate posts, and have your team collaborate on any content-related activities right inside the calendar; this feature is very useful for managing your social media presence.

4.6   Social media listening tools

Manage your social media publishing in a more effective manner by posting to various platforms with just one click if you are a social media publisher. In addition, you will get specific suggestions on the most effective times to post, allowing you to maximise both your exposure and the number of interactions your content receives.

Instruments for monitoring social media activity

Monitoring the online discussions taking place about your company is an essential step in determining the true effect of your marketing efforts, which extends beyond the number of likes and comments received.

- Social listening is monitoring social media for questions and themes, discovering conversations taking place about your company, and assessing how people feel about such talks.
- Google Alerts enables you to get frequent email updates and set up alerts for important terms and themes that arise online. This ensures that you will never miss an opportunity to mention your brand.

4.7   Social customer care tools

The employment responsibilities of social media managers have recently expanded to include the management of connections with influencers. However, it has also developed into one of the most essential responsibilities on their lists of things to accomplish. Discover the most influential people for your social media audience in a matter of seconds with our AI-powered tool that searches for influencers. You will get a quick summary of their demographics, audience size, and engagement, in addition to an easy-to-understand performance score, which will allow you to collaborate with the most influential individuals. Many of your consumers will turn to social media as their channel of choice when they want to share their feedback or inquire about your company. You may need the following in order to effectively handle all of the incoming messages:

Community management is interacting with your community in a manner that is both organized and efficient by using automatic alerts and clearly defined roles and duties for each member of the team. In order to deliver excellent customer service, you need to be able to see all incoming communications across channels in a single location and track the productivity of your teams using feeds that can be filtered.

It is essential to recognize that social media managers may not always have the ability or resources to solve every problem that develops within their community. This is an important consideration when it comes to social customer service. Therefore, it is crucial for organizations to offer them with the required assistance and resources to escalate and handle these problems swiftly and to enhance the entire experience. This will make the customer feel better overall.

4.8   Analytics tools for social media platforms

Monitoring how well your social media efforts are doing, determining which strategies are the most effective, and addressing any gaps in performance are all essential components of a successful marketing strategy. This highlights how crucial it is to have the appropriate tools at your disposal.

Analytics for social media allow you to get a comprehensive comprehension of your performance across channels with regard to all of the most important indicators, including the following:

- Participation in all aspects
- A sprinkling of different kinds of interactions
- The most interesting sorts of posts
- The actions of users
- The number of interactions for every one thousand fans
- The number of posts made by fans
- A rundown of the most interesting posts
- A portion of the interactions that were created by the promoted posts

You will also be able to evaluate how you stack up against your primary competitors with regard to these metrics in order to determine who is currently in the lead. In addition, in order to provide an even deeper level of context for your performance, you may compare the efficacy of your video marketing plan and the money you spend on advertisements to those of your sector, region, or nation. Utilize Google Analytics to learn which social media channels send the most visitors to your website.

4.9 How to manage and analyze social media audience

As was discussed earlier, doing research on the demographics and interests of your target audience should serve as the cornerstone of your social media strategy. It is necessary to have a more in-depth understanding of your community before you can proceed with the development of any content or the launch of any campaigns.

- **The first step** is to do an audience analysis. When you have more information, you will be able to construct a picture of your target market that is more accurate. You should, ideally, be utilizing software that aggregates data from many sources about your audience, since this will save you both time and human labour. A helpful hint is that certain audience information will not be accessible via the native analytics of platforms or even through Google Analytics. You might think about conducting surveys or undertaking market research if you require answers to really precise queries like "what is everyone's favourite place to travel to?"

- **The second step** is to compile information about your audience. When you retrieve the data, it is possible that it will be disorganized and difficult to understand once you do so. To gain a complete picture of the people that make up your social media network, you need to compile and examine all of the relevant data in a one location.

- **The third step** is to define the personalities of your target audience. Your audience on social media is comprised of a wide variety of individuals who fall into a variety of demographic categories and who engage in a variety of activities. You are possible to get a more in-depth insight of your personalities by dividing your audience into different groups according to the traits listed above. As a consequence of this, you will have the ability to craft content that generates engagement and successfully guides members of your community through the sales funnel.

- **The fourth step** is to conduct regular reviews of your audience personas. It is not sufficient to conduct a study of your community just once and then depend on the results for many years. Keep in mind that your audience is always shifting, as new people are beginning to follow your page and your "old" followers may start to show interest in other types of material. You need to do frequent analysis of your audience personas if you want to be able to recognize these patterns in a timely manner and take appropriate action.

4.10   How to manage social media content creation

After you have finished analyzing the audience personas you have created, you should have a general sense of the path that your content strategy ought to follow. However, choosing on content forms and themes is not the be-all and end-all of the process. As your company grows, one of the challenges you'll encounter is the problem of providing large quantities of content in a timely manner. You are going to require a content pipeline that has been optimized in order to be able to address this problem.

- **First step**: include material related to national holidays into your social media schedule. Check out Amplifies 2023 social media calendar, which details all of the important national holidays that will be celebrated throughout the year. Using this list can assist make planning for social media easier while also increasing the percentage of audience members that actively participate.
- **Step 2:** Assign roles and duties to members of the team. Dole out tasks and duties to the members of the team. Whether you work for a brand or an agency that has many offices in different locations throughout the globe, this step is essential to boosting your productivity. In

order to maximize the effectiveness of your content production, you should have the following positions on your team:

- Content manager: responsible for developing a content strategy for social media, overseeing the editorial schedule, organizing the promotion budget for content, and evaluating key performance indicators (KPIs).
- The content producer is responsible for developing ideas for relevant material, making articles that are interesting to readers, and optimizing those pieces for a variety of platforms.
- Content editor: responsible for working with everyone engaged in the development of content throughout the firm, evaluating postings, and giving the green light for them to be published.
- In addition to this, you must ensure that there is a well-defined approval procedure in place. It is simple to get mired down by confusing processes when you consider the huge volume of information that you are required to generate. Manage all of your material using a centralized system to eliminate the possibility of any of your posts being mired in the queue.
- **Third step**: Utilize the data you have collected about the personalities of your social media audience. Pay attention to the hobbies that they have and the people that they follow for influence. Using this information, you will be able to concentrate your efforts on the creation of targeted content, which will make the administration of social media much more effective overall. It is important to keep in mind that the material you provide on social media will be more successful in

achieving your company goals the more personalized it is.

- **Step 4:** Gather ideas for content via study of the competition. Gather ideas for content by researching the companies that are in direct rivalry with you, use social listening to keep track of and participate in online discussions, analyzing the pages of your personas using analytics, and collecting articles that are of interest to your audience.
- **Step 5:** Determine the frequency of your social media posts. Establish the required quantity of new material to be produced. It goes without saying that you don't want to post too little and vanish from the newsfeeds of your audience, nor do you want to write too much and seem to be spam. If you are aware of the number of posts that need to be created on a daily or weekly basis, you will be able to more effectively manage your resources and use your time.
- On Facebook, between one and two postings every day
- TikTok: between one and four postings every day
- Instagram: between one and three posts every day
- Twitter: between three and thirty updates every day
- LinkedIn: a minimum of two postings per week, with no more than one post allowed each working day
- On Pinterest, a daily pin count of between 3 and 25
- You should post one video to YouTube every week.

Step Six: Make fantastic content with the help of the many internet tools for content production that are accessible, which we covered in the previous section. Take note of the forms that function most well on each platform:

59

- Videos on Facebook (500 million people view Facebook videos every day); find out how to make the most of the video format on Facebook so you can reach your audience more effectively.
- Instagrams Reels (users spend around 20% of their time on Instagram watching Reels)
- On Twitter, tweets that include videos generate ten times more interaction than tweets that do not include videos.
- Posts on LinkedIn that include videos (your video content has the potential to garner five times more attention).

A thorough solution is required if you want to increase the output of your material while also improving the effectiveness of your labour. With Emplifi, you can effortlessly manage all of the material that you post to your social network accounts on a daily, weekly, or monthly basis. You will be able to save time by instructing your team to plan and publish items from inside the calendar. These postings may include photographs, videos, and mentions of other users.

Step 7: Track how well social material is doing and submit your findings.

Track the performance of your content and produce a report on it. Monitoring the degree to which your personas respond to your postings gives you the ability to determine which aspects of your campaign are the most successful and to direct your efforts and resources towards recreating those aspects in the future. The following is a list of metrics that you need to be tracking:

- Metrics for awareness include an overview of engagement, the amount of interactions for every 1,000 followers, and the best-performing posts
- Accomplishment of the campaign's goals, including link clicks, sign-ups, and sales

Dashboards that may be customized allow for instantaneous data analysis of the parameters in question. Use automatic reports that are sent directly to the inboxes of team members at whatever frequency you deem necessary in order to ensure that your team is always up to date on the most recent data.

4.11   How to manage social media listening

Listening to conversations on social media platforms is an essential part of running a social media management operation. Performing this action on a consistent basis may facilitate the completion of a variety of tasks, including the following:

- Keeping an eye on mentions on social media and how your initiatives are doing there
- Investigating what individuals are saying about your competition on social media platforms
- Providing superior care for the customers
- Finding new people to act as brand ambassadors and social media influencers
- Recognizing and avoiding any potential social media problems relating to the brand
- Identifying more general discussions in which your company should participate

First step, choose the appropriate keywords to use in your query. You will need to choose the appropriate phrases that you want to concentrate on in order to fulfil the objective that you have set for yourself. For instance, if your objective is to identify potential influencers via listening, you should get started by generating inquiries connected to the subject of your campaign. Create a list of the relevant keywords, hashtags, and mentions you wish to monitor and include it in the query. In the last step, choose the platform that you want to monitor, as well as the default language and area. As a consequence of this, you will be able to get precisely the information that is of interest to you.

Step 2: Pay attention and make observations. After deciding on the terms you want to watch, utilize a social media listening tool to begin keeping an eye on how they are being discussed. The following are some of the many applications that might be made of the information that you will obtain:

- Campaign monitoring: pay attention to what people are talking about your company and its content, and then join the discussion in order to boost user participation.
- Competitive intelligence is observing how individuals react to the information provided by your rivals and analyzing the volume and tone of those individuals' answers in order to derive conclusions that may be acted upon and incorporated into your own strategy.
- High-caliber customer service: monitor incoming inquiries and feedback and be prepared to provide a response as soon as possible in order to boost client satisfaction and improve the image of your business.
- Brand champions and influencers: get an understanding of who is talking about your company so that you may capitalize on the powerful voices of those individuals to reach new audiences.

- Managing a crisis requires prompt identification of complaints and critical feedback in order to forestall the escalation of existing disagreements.
- Check to see whether the keywords or brand references you're using have any connotations attached to them. This will assist you in understanding the context of debates revolving around your brand and will allow you to make comments that are more educated.

4.12 How to manage social media influencers

The management of connections with influential people used to fall within the purview of public relations firms not so long ago. However, because of the rise in popularity of influencer marketing, working together with influencers has become an essential component of social media management. The popularity of influencer marketing is growing, which is driving the worldwide market for influencer marketing to see fast expansion. The size of the market is projected to reach a huge 22.2 billion U.S. dollars by the year 2025, according to the projections that have been made. This chore has, thankfully, grown considerably simpler as a result of the proliferation of end-to-end solutions for managing influencers. Let's have a look at how to construct an effective plan for marketing using influencers:

Step 1: Define your goals and KPIs. To begin defining objectives and key performance indicators for a social influencer program, you should:

- Making sure that your goals are very clear.
- Determining who your ideal customers are and being familiar with their demographics and areas of interest.

- Transforming your objectives into concrete targets that can be measured, such as an increase in the proportion of people who follow you on social media or mentions of your company.
- Choosing appropriate Key Performance Indicators (KPIs) that match with your aims and ensuring that they can be assessed successfully.

Using this method, you will be able to monitor the development of your social influencer programmer and assess its level of success.

The following are some of the most common objectives for influencer marketing:

- Increasing brand awareness by increasing the amount of social shares, mentions of the brand, earned media, reach, direct traffic, and brand searches
- Increasing sales, including the number of sales qualified leads (SQLs), items or services that have been purchased

Reaching new market segments may be defined as the number of people who are not your typical audience personas who engage with your content, sees your website, and buys your goods or services.

Step 2: Determine which individuals are the most influential to your target demographic. Working with someone only due to the fact that they are very well-known or have already collaborated with a number of different worldwide businesses is not a good idea. Instead, you should concentrate on finding someone who is the ideal fit for your audience, even if they are a specialized group. The question now is, how do you locate the influencers that your audience respects?

- Make use of an AI-based search engine for influencers: Avoid time-consuming human research and let AI come up with a list of prominent social media influencers that are the ideal match for each of your target profiles.
- Make use of social media listening: Find out who is already talking about your brand or discussing the terms that are relevant to your company or sector. The next step is to determine whether or not a productive partnership with the influencer is possible by examining the degree to which the influencer's audience personas align with your own.

Third Step Understanding the performance of the influencers. Reviewing a person's performance using analytics may help you determine whether or not you are teaming up with someone who is not just a good fit for your needs but also productive. It is important to pay attention to indicators like engagement and follower growth as well as the efficiency of sponsored articles since they will give you a sense of how successful the influencer is.

Step 4: Become familiar with the influential person. Discuss your objectives, your expectations, and the ideas you have for the campaign with them, and let the influencer to do the same. Your ability to collaborate effectively with the influencer will be directly correlated to the amount of campaign specifics that you supply. Find out how to successfully create connections with social media influencers and use that information to your advantage.

Fifth step work on a content strategy. The majority of marketers make the error of trying to coerce influencers into using certain content forms, subjects, or publication frequency. In point of fact, however, the influencers are the ones who need to be choosing the ultimate form that the campaign will take. After all, they are the ones who are most knowledgeable about how to meaningfully connect their consumers. Utilize our blog, which focuses on the unrealized potential of influencer marketing, as a source of inspiration for your next influencer marketing campaign.

Sixth step is to evaluate your performance. You need to keep a careful eye on your performance for the whole of the campaign in order to determine how successful your influencer partnership really is. Don't forget to compare the return on investment (ROI) of your influencer campaign to the ROI of your other digital marketing initiatives; doing so will help you to assess how cost-effective your influencer partnership was.

4.13   How to manage social media customer care
Providing outstanding customer service via social media is essential to attracting and keeping a dedicated and active audience. A company's income is another aspect that is directly influenced by it. Statista estimates that sixty percent of the world's population is actively participating in some kind of social media. To effectively interact with one's clientele, it is necessary for every company to develop and execute a social media strategy. Because of this, providing excellent customer service via social media is essential. Now let's take a look at the ways in which your team may deliver excellent customer service using social media:

- **Step 1:** Make a list of the channels where your clients communicate with you the most often so that you can concentrate your efforts, both in terms of time and resources, on monitoring these platforms.
- **Step 2:** Assign tasks and duties to the staff that will be caring for your social media customers. You are able to choose a specific individual to handle each platform or category of inquiries (for instance, queries about the technical aspects of a product might be handled separately from complaints). It is also a good idea to have one person oversee all of the customer service operations. This individual should be responsible for ensuring that the replies are suitable and approving the messages that are sent out.
- **Step 3**: Establish criteria for providing service to customers. If you do this, you will be able to maintain coherence in your replies and make sure they are in line with the voice of your business. Should you project an image of friendliness or one of professionalism? Should you follow up with queries asked in the comment area or send them a direct message instead? Should you actively participate in discussions with your consumers, even if the topics being discussed have nothing to do with your company? These are only some of the questions that may be answered with the assistance of a style guide.
- **Step 4:** involves monitoring social media and keeping an ear out for queries, comments, and mentions of the company. You should try to respond to as many customers as possible every day in order to provide timely assistance, participate in discussions while they are still relevant, and identify potential issues before

they arise. In the event that a crisis does grow, however, it is important to maintain composure and read our article on how to handle a crisis on social media.

- **Step 5:** Give a report on how well you did. In the same way that you should regularly evaluate your other social media marketing operations, your customer service should also be evaluated often. Reporting on the performance of your customer service in terms of the sorts of questions you are being asked or the average amount of time it takes you to respond will enable you to find gaps and address any deficiencies.

4.14   How to handle the monitoring and reporting of social media activity

A data-driven approach should form the basis of any social media plan that is intended to be effective, including the choices surrounding financial expenditures. It is essential to have a solid understanding of the profitability of spending money on social media marketing in light of the fact that more and more cash is being put into this endeavour. Monitoring and reporting become important at precisely this point in the process. By engaging in these two activities, you will have an understanding of how the financial resources dedicated to social media are affecting the bottom line of your company. They also make it possible for you to rapidly change your plan; the sooner you acquire the data on your performance, the quicker you'll be able to grow better. Keeping the appropriate focus is essential to accurate monitoring and reporting. You will be able to assess your performance more accurately if you are aware of the precise breadth of the data that you need in order to be able to make conclusions that are actionable. When assessing the many aspects of social media, the following metrics are the ones you should focus on paying attention to:

- An examination of the audience, including its size, demographics, interests, and behaviours, as well as its personas (however it should be noted that personas will evolve over time).
- Content performance including reach, engagement overview, engagement type breakdown, number of interactions per 1,000 followers, top-performing articles, click-through rate, and referral traffic
- Listening on social media involves monitoring the amount and frequency of mentions of a brand, as well as the mood and influencers who discuss the brand.
- Influencer marketing: an overview of influencers that match your audience personas, as well as their demographics, interests, audience size, interactions, number of posts, and hashtags they're using; to track the influencer's campaign performance, zoom in on their reach, engagement overview, number of interactions per 1,000 fans, CTR, and volume of referral traffic;
- Metrics for advertisements: click-through rate, cost per thousand impressions, cost per click, reach, and frequency
- Customer service via social media: the number of comments, queries, and complaints received from customers; sentiment; response times on average

You should evaluate yourself in relation to the other companies in your industry so that you can give your monitoring more depth. For instance, in terms of the increase of followers, engagement, or the effectiveness of the investments made in social media. You will have a clearer idea of where you are as a result, and you will have the ability to adjust your plan appropriately should the need arise. When it comes to reporting, it is essential to keep your scope limited, be succinct, and make sure that your data tells a narrative. Finding the optimal frequency is also very important. You should report with your team once every month, and you should report with upper management once every three months as a general rule of thumb. Make sure you plan automatic reports to be sent to your email inbox on a weekly basis so that you can keep a close eye on your progress towards achieving your objectives.

Step 1: you'll need to define the variables that will be used in your social media report. You have to get the answers to these three significant questions before you can even begin to create a report:

- For whom is this report being prepared?
- For what period of time does your report cover social media activity?
- What kind of research did you do to compile your study on social media?

Step 2: Determine which indicators will be most useful for your social media report. You should give some thought to the narrative you want to convey as well as the metrics that most accurately represent the effect of the social media activities you do.

Step 3: Compare your results to those of the other companies in your industry. This stage is essential since it provides your report with a larger framework in which to be understood. When it comes to improving your ability to handle social media, having more knowledge on how you compare to your rivals is a helpful advice that you can use. In addition to this, it sends a message to your management that you do in-depth analysis of your data and look at more than just your personal performance.

Step 4: Compare your results to those of other companies in the same sector, nation, and area. By doing so, you will be able to determine if any performance changes are unique to you or whether they are the consequence of a larger event, such as an increase in seasonal traffic or modifications to the algorithm used to generate newsfeeds.

4.15   Conclusion

It may seem to be difficult to manage social media, but this is not the case if you have the appropriate procedures and tools in place. You will be able to conduct your digital marketing operations and accomplish your company objectives much more effectively if you follow the steps that are mentioned in this article and use the assistance of complete social media marketing and management solutions such as those that are offered by Emplifi.

Chapter No. 05

Social Media Marketing Platforms for 2024

The number of global social media users have been increasing steadily for the past decade, and it's predicted to reach almost 4.4 billion by 2025. Leading social networks like Facebook, Instagram, LinkedIn, Twitter, etc. have reshaped the lives of people at large. The way we communicate, exchange content, and spend time on the internet have changed significantly.

Not only did it transform our social interactions, but it has also impacted how brands approach marketing. Marketers have now found a new channel to connect and engage with their target audience, while businesses use social networking sites to promote their products.

Considering that there are more than 200 active social media websites, it's a challenging job, though, for businesses to maintain their presence on all the leading social networking sites actively. Even if they want to use only a few social networking platforms (let's say only the top 5), it's still a big task. For this reason, marketers and brands often turn to social media marketing platforms. With the help of one of the following tools, you can make your social media marketing more effective and profitable without having to sacrifice your own social life.

5.1   Brandwatch Social Media Management

Brandwatch is a social media marketing platform that offers a solution for marketers that want to inspire on social media. It offers weekly training sessions and real-time in-app chat, email, and telephone service. Brandwatch offers dedicated support on your daily workflows or social media strategy.

Key Features:

- A content calendar and campaign planner
- Advanced analytics dashboards
- Community management and in-app support
- Social media advertising and competitor benchmark (Full Suite only)

5.2 Loomly

If you're working as part of a bigger team, Loomly is a good choice as it focuses a lot on streamlining team management and its end-to-end post and ad history will ensure that every team member is on the same page. Trusted by thousands of marketing teams around the globe, they've helped global names like BMW, Porsche, and L'Oréal build their brands. It offers a long list of features to simplify brand and content management that includes tools like a central asset library, hashtag manager, and automatically generated post and ad previews.

Key Features:

- Automated publishing – Facebook, Twitter, Instagram, Pinterest, LinkedIn, and Google My Business
- Analytics for all posts
- Custom post ideas
- Approval workflow and a commenting system

5.3 Sendible

It is a multi-purpose social media management tool that does a lot of things. Sendible lets you manage multiple social media accounts, collaborate with your social media marketing team, and monitor brand mentions.

Key Features:

- An all-in-one social media marketing platform.
- You can create a social media marketing strategy with Sendible easily.
- Powerful reporting simplifies tracking and analysis.

5.4   Birdeye

Birdeye's platform leverages AI-powered content generation to create engaging, industry-specific social media posts complemented by contextually relevant images. It offers a unified solution for multi-location social media management, enabling businesses to efficiently publish, engage, and analyze across platforms like Facebook, Instagram, LinkedIn, YouTube, and Google. The platform's insightful analytics measure content performance, social reach, and engagement by location, equipping businesses with data to refine their social media strategies.

Key Features:

- Social Publishing
- Visual Calendar
- Social Scheduling
- Instant Notifications
- Social Reporting
- Centralized Inbox
- Post Tracking

5.5   Planoly

Trusted and loved by 5+ million users, Planoly is a comprehensive platform to schedule your content on Instagram, Pinterest, Twitter, and Facebook. As an official Pinterest and Instagram partner, it's especially useful if you mostly post on these two channels.

Key Features:

- It offers powerful web and mobile apps.
- You can use it to access basic and advanced analytics.
- For improved engagement, it shares suggestions for the best time to post.
- It has a wide range of image filters, designer templates, and stickers to help you create content.

5.6   Brand24

It is another brand reputation management tool that is specifically designed to work with social networks. Brand24 tracks your brand mention on social networking websites, notifies you immediately, and lets you analyze how satisfied your customers are.

Key Features:

- It is a powerful tool suitable for teams.
- It monitors sentiment analysis.
- You can measure customer satisfaction with Brand24 too.

5.7   HeyOrca

HeyOrca stands as an exemplar in the landscape of social media marketing platforms, setting itself apart through innovative features and user-centric design tailored to the dynamic needs of agencies. Efficiency and synergy are at the core of HeyOrca offering, allowing teams to centralize social media management, streamline content creation, and enhance client engagement through an intuitive interface.

Key Features:

- Centralized Calendar
- Event Strips
- Copy Post
- Approvals
- HeyOrca Reports

5.8   Agorapulse

Agorapulse is another social media management tool for marketers that comes with a lot of features and is suitable for businesses of all sizes. You can use it to manage all social media accounts, communicate with your followers, engage, and increase your followers. Its built-in CRM is a perfect platform to understand and engage with your followers.

Key Features:

- A multi-purpose social media management tool.
- Works perfectly for teams.
- Supports all the leading social media networks.

5.9   Iconosquare

Iconosquare is an analytics tool that also caters to social media management, monitoring, and scheduling. As a result, Iconosquare delivers some of the most in-depth analytics we have ever seen. The main differences between its three pricing tiers (Pro, Advanced, and Enterprise) relate to the number of social profiles you can monitor, the number of hashtags and competitors you can observe, and the number of team members who can access your account.

The higher plans also add a few additional capabilities, such as custom dashboards and PDF reports (company branded in the case of Enterprise).

Key Features:

- Advanced analytics – Instagram, Facebook, Twitter, and LinkedIn
- Multi-profile management from one dashboard – Instagram, Facebook, and Twitter
- Powerful scheduler – Instagram, Facebook, and Twitter
- Insightful industry benchmarks for over 100 industries – Instagram and Facebook

5.10   PromoRepublic

PromoRepublic was initially launched as a social media platform for small businesses. Fast-forward eight years and they've become one of the leading social media marketing platforms for brands. It offers a great scheduling feature that makes it easy to post your business page. Pair that with its ready-to-use post templates and relevant graphics and maintaining and growing your social media presence become a whole lot easier.

Key Features:

- Automated posting – Facebook, Twitter, Instagram, Pinterest, LinkedIn, and Google My Business
- Built-in graphics editor
- An efficient workflow setup
- User-friendly reports

5.11   Audiense

Audience lets you understand your audience better and is similar to Social bakers. However, its Audiense Connect is the Twitter marketing platform that is specifically developed for social media marketing. It lets you connect, manage, and grow your Twitter community. The insights will help you improve Twitter performance significantly.

Key Features:

- A Twitter chatbot is great for boosting engagement.
- It segments your Twitter audience to improve targeting.
- You can grow your followers with its powerful analytics.

5.12 NapoleonCat

Founded in 2013, NapoleonCat is trusted by the likes of Allianz, OLX, and the WWF and boasts glowing reviews on review sites like GetApp and Capterra. After you've viewed its interface, you'll understand why. It just looks better than you've probably grown used to. Though, it's not all about looks and when it comes to user experience, it also delivers. Getting started is straightforward and its Social Inbox will blow you away. Here, you'll find everything you'll need to streamline customer engagement and care.

Key Features:

- You can use it to handle generic comments automatically.
- Its performance analytics lets you measure and analyze your progress on the major platforms.
- It has an Instagram Scheduler for scheduling and publishing content automatically.

5.13 Visme

If you want to create infographics, presentations, GIFs, charts, or any other type of social media graphics, Visme is the best social media marketing platform tool for it. Visme comes with a simple dashboard, templates, and a huge library of graphics and photos to make your life easier. The best thing about Visme is that it lets you create infographics even if you aren't a designer.

Key Features:

- It has a huge collection of assets for its users.
- You can create several types of visual content.
- It lets you collect and store leads.

5.14   Buffer

A social media scheduling tool is one of the most essential tools for social media marketers. You have to make sure you post the right content at the right time and this is what Buffer does exceptionally well. It is a social media scheduling tool that lets you publish, interact, and analyze social media progress for all the leading social platforms.

Key Features:

- It is free to use with limited features.
- It supports all the leading social networks.
- Chrome extension is a lifesaver.

5.15   Pablo

If you are using Buffer, you must use Pablo. It lets you create photos in 30 seconds that you can share via Buffer. It has a drag-and-drop user interface that has a lot of templates to help you get started. The best part: You can convert text to an image with a single click.

Key Features:

- It is absolutely free to use.

- It has a Chrome extension that lets you convert text into an image with a single mouse-click.
- The user-interface is fairly easy-to-use.

5.16 ContentCal

Although ContentCal initially began as a social media marketing agency and then developed a platform focusing on scheduling and publishing, it has since extended its focus to planning, collaborating, analyzing, and storing content. It includes in-built approval flows to help streamline the process and avoid bottlenecks. It is affordable, with plans ranging from $37/mo. or $30/mo. when billed annually.

Key Features:

- It has a visual calendar to plan, create, and share marketing content
- You can create template posts, save ideas, and store images, media, and links in one central content hub
- Automatically publish your content to multiple platforms at your chosen time and date
- Automatically schedule content to multiple platforms

5.17 Sprout Social

Sprout Social is an all-in-one social media management tool. It offers you several features to understand and reach your audience and to engage with your followers. Sprout Social supports Facebook, Twitter, Instagram, LinkedIn, and Pinterest. It has a social CRM tool that helps you manage the relationship with your followers.

Key Features:

- It comes with a social calendar.

- It has paid promotion tools that help you with social ads.
- It offers you with powerful analytics.

5.18 Onlypult

Not only can you use OnlyPult to post on social media platforms, but you can also use it to post to your blog as well. It includes an extensive collection of well-integrated features, and we can only touch the surface in this post. Plans start at $25/mo., but they offer a free no credit card 7-day trial. OnlyPult is a quick and easy-to-use tool with more features than your average social media marketing software.

Key Features:

- You can post in multiple ways across Facebook, Instagram, Twitter, LinkedIn, Google My Business, YouTube, TikTok, Tumblr, WordPress, Telegram, Vkontakte, Odnoklassniki, Pinterest, and Medium. It includes auto scheduling and multi-posting.
- It includes Builder, a link-in-bio tool that lets you create micro landing pages that link to other assets.
- It includes a social media listening/monitoring tool for crisis management and improving your customer satisfaction.

5.19 Later

If you are a fan of Instagram, you'll love using Later. Though it works for other social networks too, Instagram marketing is its core specialty. You can visually plan and schedule Instagram posts. It has a powerful organizer that lets you organize your Instagram photos and posts.

Key Features:

- It has a free plan for individual users.
- You can create clickable landing pages to boost conversions.
- Choose from unlimited media for your posts.

5.20   Followerwonk

If Twitter is your company's primary social network, don't miss Followerwonk. It has multiple tools to supercharge Twitter marketing for your business. It helps you find appropriate Twitter accounts, lets you compare accounts, and analyze followers.

Key Features

- Compare Twitter accounts to find influencers.
- Segment followers based on several variables.
- Compare your relationship with your competitors.

5.21   Tailwind

Tailwind is a social media marketing app that works for Pinterest and Instagram. It is primarily used as a scheduling app, but it has other features too. For instance, it helps you find the best time to post on Instagram with its Smart Schedule feature.

Key Features:

- You can find hashtags with a single click.
- It lets you create multiple pins with a single click.
- It has powerful analytics that helps you with growth.

5.22   Tagboard

Tagboard is an interesting and useful tool for social media management and marketing. You can find social media posts that can be aggregated and curated easily. A simple hashtag can reveal several social media stories that are all public. You can then republish them on your social media account.

Key Features:

- It works as a complete reputation management tool.
- You can find trending content on any topic.
- It can be integrated with Hootsuite.

5.23   BuzzSumo

BuzzSumo is an awesome tool that helps you find popular content that's trending on social networking sites. You can identify trending content that people like and share on your preferred social network and recreate it. It also helps you find influencers who publish or share content that's relevant to your business.

Key Features:

- It is a powerful tool for content discovery.
- You can find keywords, content ideas, and titles that people love sharing.
- It improves engagement by letting you monitor and respond to comments.

5.24   Mention

Social listening goes hand in hand with social media marketing. Mention is the best tool for managing your brand's reputation by actively listening to what people are saying about your business on social networking sites.

Key Features:

- You can add and track social accounts.

- Active social media monitoring.
- Its sentiment analysis feature is just amazing.

5.25 Emplifi

Emplifi is an AI-powered tool that helps you understand your audience on social media. You can use insights to create better content for your audience. It offers multiple solutions and advanced features that significantly improve social media marketing.

Key Features

- It is a perfect tool to create buyer personas
- You can create and manage social content strategy
- It helps you run and manage influencer marketing campaigns

5.26 Tweepi

If you are struggling with Twitter marketing and find it hard to grow your followers, you should use Tweepi. It is a perfect tool for businesses that want to engage with their Twitter followers. It uses AI to find tweets and accounts that are more likely to engage and follow you.

Key Features:

- It works automatically.
- You can gain over 100 new followers every day with it.
- You can connect with your target audience without any hassle.

5.27 Feedly

Feedly keeps your information organized. You can add sources that you are interested in. The rest will be handled by feedly. It will make it super-easy to read and share relevant material. This helps you in finding, organizing, and managing content for social media. You can share new content every single day with your audience with the help of feedly.

Key Features:

- It filters the content based on your preferences.
- You have always something interesting to share on your social accounts.
- You can use feedly on all types of devices seamlessly.

5.28   Lumen5

Video content works best on social networking sites especially if you are using Instagram. Lumen5 is a great tool that helps you create videos with its straight-forward dashboard. There are tons of templates to help you get started immediately. You can create a video in less than a minute from any blog post you have. The video format, length, and dimensions are set based on the social network you create it for.

Key Features:

- Text to video is the best feature that lets you convert text into video.
- It has a huge library of images, music, and video clips to make your videos professional.
- Text position is adjusted by the AI tool and the appropriate keywords are automatically highlighted.

5.29   Zapier

How could you miss Zapier? It is a simple free tool that automates workflows by connecting and integrating apps. You can connect your CRM, lead generation tool, email marketing software, and other tools with social networking sites for automating several tasks.

Key Features:

- Zapier takes automation to a whole new level.
- It works with all the leading apps and tools.
- It increases productivity by making your social media marketing effective.

5.30   Canva

Canva is a free drag-and-drop design tool that is a must-have for marketers and businesses. You can create professional images for social media posts. It has a huge library of templates, photos, icons, shapes, graphs, and more that can be used by anyone to create a perfect social media post.

Key Features:

- It is free-to-use.
- The interface is exceptionally easy with no learning curve.
- It has a huge collection of graphics for its users.

5.31   SocialPilot

SocialPilot offers powerful publishing and scheduling features, along with the analytics that you need to optimize your social media strategy. And, if you're serious about scaling your social media efforts, it also lets you bulk schedule up to 500 posts with a single upload. As any experienced social media manager would tell you, it's not all about posting content, though. You also need to engage with your audience and to help you with this part of the job, you can use its basic, but effective, Social Inbox that combines all your comments, messages, and Instagram Story replies.

Key Features:

- You can assign specific roles and access rules to different team members.
- You can customize social media reports with your own branding.
- You can search content for unlimited keywords.

5.32   e-clincher

Founded in 2012, eclincher offers a comprehensive social media management tool that can help you with key tasks like publishing, scheduling, content curation, and analytics. It's integrated with the top social networks (TikTok isn't currently part of its integrations, but it's coming soon). On the topic of new features, it recently introduced reputation management and brand monitoring. So, not only can you now engage with your audience via its all-in-one Smart Inbox, but you can also find out how consumers really feel about your business thanks to its sentiment analysis functionality.

Key Features:

- You can get instant access to brand mentions.
- You can use the drag-and-drop functionality to plan your posts visually.
- You can merge your social channels into a single feed.

5.33   Hootsuite

It's hard to manage multiple social media accounts on all the top social networking sites. Hootsuite solves this issue by letting you manage all the social accounts (Facebook,

Instagram, Twitter, LinkedIn, YouTube and Pinterest) from a single dashboard. Instead of visiting all the social networking sites individually, you can log in to your Hootsuite account and manage all of them. This includes creating posts, scheduling posts, content curation, account management, and more.

Key Features:

- It supports all the leading social networks (Facebook, Instagram, Twitter, LinkedIn, YouTube and Pinterest).
- You can monitor all social accounts from a single dashboard.
- It helps you create and schedule posts to various networks at the same time.
- You can view upcoming scheduled content and collaborate in real time with team members.
- It lets you measure how your posts perform across all the networks and create customized reports.

5.34   Social Champ

Social Champ caters to marketers aiming for streamlined social media management. The platform touts its ability to simplify the task of handling multiple social accounts, making content organization and analysis a breeze. It provides a vast array of features, designed to cater to marketers' myriad needs.

Key Features:

- Publishing Capabilities
- Robust Social Media Calendar
- In-Depth Analytics
- Unified Engagement Interface

- Integrations

5.35 Zoho Social

Zoho Social provides a user-friendly experience for brands aiming to manage their social media presence effectively. It offers tools that save time and increase efficiency in scheduling posts, tracking performance, and engaging with the audience. The platform is designed to serve both businesses and agencies.

Key Features:

- Flexible Scheduling
- Intuitive Content Calendar
- Active Monitoring Dashboard
- Comprehensive Social Analytics
- Instagram Integration
- Mobile Management

Social media marketing platforms help your business in several ways, but you have to understand that it isn't all about tools. The way you use these tools is important. Having a lot of tools in your marketing stack doesn't ensure success. A robust social media marketing strategy is what's essential for success.

Chapter No. 05

Advantages and disadvantages of social media marketing

Instead of relying on traditional advertising methods, businesses now embrace a more interactive, dynamic and customer-centric approach social media marketing. It has revolutionized how businesses reach out to their target audience. The true magic of social media marketing lies in its capacity to reach millions of customers with a single post — first by capturing their attention and then transforming them into followers and eventually customers. In fact, research indicates that 76% of consumers make purchasing decisions after encountering a product-related post on social media platforms.

On average, individuals spend over 2 hours and 29 minutes browsing social media. This emphasizes the need for businesses to establish a presence on these platforms so as to form meaningful connections with consumers. But, like any marketing strategy, social media marketing also has its pros and cons.

6.1   Advantages of social media marketing
Let's begin with the advantages of social media marketing.

6.1.1   Cost-effective advertising
Social media platforms like Facebook, Instagram, Twitter, YouTube and LinkedIn provide affordable advertising options to reach out to a wider audience. With features like targeted advertising, you can make the most of your

marketing dollars and achieve a higher return on investment (ROI).

6.1.2 Building brand loyalty

Social media platforms help you better engage with your customers. You can make them feel heard by responding to their comments and addressing their concerns promptly. This helps in building trust and creating a sense of community. When your consumers feel valued, they will turn into brand advocates and spread positive word-of-mouth recommendations.

6.1.3 Influencer partnerships

Today, more than 50% of millennials trust influencers' product recommendations. By partnering with influencers who align with your brand values, you can leverage their credibility to promote your products or services. This will help boost brand visibility and potential customer acquisition.

6.1.4 Audience insights and market research

Social media platforms provide valuable insights into audience demographics, interests and behavior. In fact, more than 64% of business owners use social media data to gather insights into their customer's requirements and online behavior.

By analyzing social media data, businesses can gain a deeper understanding of their target audience, identify emerging trends and stay ahead of the competition. These insights can be used to tailor marketing campaigns and develop products or services that cater to specific needs.

6.1.5   Viral marketing opportunities

Social media has the power to make your content go viral and help you reach a massive audience within a short time. Through creative campaigns, compelling storytelling and user-generated content, you can increase your chances of creating viral marketing moments, leading to exponential growth in brand awareness and engagement.

6.1.6   Enhanced customer targeting and segmentation

Social media platforms enable businesses to segment their audience and target specific customer segments with tailored social media messaging. By understanding the different needs, preferences and behaviors of various customer segments, you can create customized content that resonates with each group. This increases customer engagement, enhances their overall experience and increases conversions.

6.1.7   Access to user-generated content

Social media platforms offer a wealth of user-generated content that can be harnessed by businesses. Showcasing customer photos, sharing positive reviews and running user-generated content campaigns can build trust, credibility and authenticity.

6.1.8   Competitive advantage

A strong social media presence gives your business a competitive edge. By actively engaging with customers, providing timely responses and staying up-to-date on the latest industry trends, companies can position themselves as industry leaders.

6.1.9   Global reach and localization

Social media breaks down geographical barriers, enabling businesses to reach a global audience. These platforms also offer localization options, allowing your company to target specific regions, languages or cultural nuances. Although social media marketing is of great strategic importance, it also has some pitfalls that a business should always keep in mind.

6.1.10   You Have Access to Paid Advertising Services

The customizable nature of social media platforms makes them an appealing marketing tool. You can set your target demographic on several of them, for example. You may then track the effectiveness of your advertisements. Using social media ads marketing settings, you can target consumers based on their gender, age, education, career, family status, lifestyle, online behavior, interest in your competitor's products, and other factors.

If you can't monitor the efficacy of your ads, you won't be able to enhance your reach. The good thing about marketing on popular platforms is that it allows you to track how well your ad campaigns perform. Furthermore, these social media advertising campaigns are significantly less expensive than typical Google ads.

6.1.11   You Can Evaluate Your Performance

When you run a social media marketing campaign, you want to know how well it performs. You can quickly track your campaign's performance on social media networks to see if it's delivering results. It is possible to see how many people have seen your posts and how many have left comments, liked them, shared them, and so on. You may also monitor its stats if you run a social media advertising campaign. You'll see analytics such as impressions, clicks, and conversions. It is also possible to check how many people viewed your posts, comments, likes, shares, and more. If you can evaluate the performance of your social media plan, you can adapt and improve it.

6.2 Disadvantages of social media marketing
Now, let's discuss some of the cons of social media marketing.

6.2.1 Time and resource intensive
Maintaining an effective social media presence requires a significant investment of time and resources. Creating and curating engaging content, managing multiple social media platforms, maintaining a consistent brand experience and responding to customer inquiries demand continuous effort and a dedicated team. Without proper planning and allocation of resources, social media marketing efforts can become overwhelming and less effective and lead to a dip in the quality of the content.

6.2.2 Negative feedback and reputation management
Negative comments or reviews can quickly spread across social media platforms, potentially damaging a company's reputation. A single negative incident or social media backlash can significantly impact a company's reputation. Effective social media crisis management and proactive reputation monitoring are vital to managing the impact of negative viral content.

6.2.3 Changes in platform algorithm
Social media platforms frequently update their algorithms, affecting the reach and visibility of organic content. These

algorithm changes can significantly impact a business's social media strategy. You must stay updated on platform changes and adjust your approach to maintain visibility and engagement with your audience.

6.2.4 Information overload and limited attention span

With users scrolling through endless posts, it becomes crucial for businesses to create compelling and visually appealing content that can cut through the noise. An internet user, on average, is bombarded with almost 4,000 and 10,000 ads every day. Due to this, your social media marketing efforts can lead to little returns because it is becoming increasingly difficult to capture a user's attention.

6.2.5 Return on investment measurement

While social media platforms offer analytics tools to track metrics, such as engagement, reach and website traffic, tying these metrics directly to revenue generation can be challenging. Attribution models and tracking mechanisms must be implemented to accurately evaluate the impact of social media marketing on business goals.

6.2.6 Privacy and data security concerns

Social media platforms collect vast amounts of user data, raising privacy and data security concerns. You must handle and use this data responsibly. Any misuse of consumer data can lead to your company facing legal consequences. This can damage its reputation, which might take years to rebuild.

6.2.7 Qualified Staff Are Needed

If you want to focus on your important business matters, we highly recommend that you hire staff. Your staff will be able to create your content and run your social media accounts. But, you need them to be competent and able to do the work. Using social media for business purposes isn't the same as when it's for personal accounts. You will likely have to provide your staff with the right tools, internet connection and whatever else they may need. Naturally, you'll have to pay them decent wages as well, which could be costly if your team is big.

6.2.8 Goals

You need to have goals and they need to make sense for your business. When it comes to digital marketing, there is no 'one-size-fits-all' solution. You need to use social media in a way that is sensible and logical. Just going out there and posting memes or funny videos won't get you very far. When you come up with your marketing plans, you need to know what results you want for your business. Do you want better brand loyalty? Are you hoping to boost awareness and offer more engaging customer service? Whatever your business goals are, be realistic. We suggest that you start with small objectives. You can gradually build on them and create more goals as your social media following grows. Give yourself time to learn what works for your customers and what doesn't.

6.2.9 Content

Our need to create and curate content that will interest your customers. You have to come up with content that they want to view and it needs to be interesting. Do market research about your audience. Find out what is important to them. Is it customer service? Then focus on creating content that addresses your relationship with your customers. If they want to know more about how your kind of product or service works, share detailed information with them. The content you share has to be 99% about your audience and 10% about your brand.

When you create content that makes your audience feel valued and involved, you will improve brand loyalty – always a good thing. You don't have to create all your content yourself, you can curate content from other sources. As long as it's relevant and reliable, you can use anything. Of course, there are some rules to follow but it's not too complicated. There you have it – the advantages and disadvantages of social media marketing. It is very easy to get started. It is also easy to get carried away and start making mistakes.

But as long as you have a well-thought-out plan and stick to it, you'll see only the benefits of social media.

Conclusion

Social media marketing has revolutionized the way businesses and individuals connect, engage, and promote their products or services. In today's digital age, it has become an essential component of any comprehensive marketing strategy. This article will explore the key aspects of social media marketing, its significance, and its impact on businesses. Social media marketing refers to the use of various social media platforms, such as Facebook, Instagram, Twitter, LinkedIn, and Pinterest, to promote products, services, or ideas. It involves creating and sharing content with the goal of reaching and engaging a target audience. This can encompass a wide range of activities, from posting text, images, and videos to running paid advertising campaigns on these platforms.

One of the primary reasons social media marketing is crucial is its unparalleled reach and accessibility. Platforms like Facebook and Instagram boast billions of active users, providing businesses with a vast and diverse audience to connect with. This makes it an ideal channel for promoting products or services, building brand awareness, and fostering customer loyalty. Furthermore, social media marketing offers a level of engagement and interaction that traditional marketing methods cannot match. It enables businesses to directly communicate with their audience, receive feedback, and address customer concerns promptly. This fosters a sense of trust and connection that is invaluable in today's competitive market.

Social media marketing is also cost-effective. Compared to traditional advertising methods, such as print or television, running ads on social media platforms is significantly cheaper. This makes it accessible to businesses of all sizes, from startups to multinational corporations. Small businesses, in particular, can benefit from the ability to target their marketing efforts to specific demographics, increasing the return on investment.

In addition to reach and cost-effectiveness, social media marketing offers a wealth of data and insights. Social media platforms provide analytics tools that allow businesses to track the performance of their marketing campaigns. This data includes metrics like engagement, click-through rates, and conversion rates, which enable businesses to make data-driven decisions and refine their marketing strategies for better results.

The power of social media marketing extends beyond just selling products. It also plays a crucial role in building and maintaining a brand's reputation. Businesses can use social media to establish their brand identity, share their values, and showcase their expertise in their industry. Through consistent and engaging content, they can create a loyal community of followers who become advocates for their brand. However, social media marketing is not without its challenges. The digital landscape is constantly evolving, and algorithms change frequently. It can be challenging to keep up with the latest trends and ensure that content reaches the intended audience. Moreover, the potential for negative feedback and public relations crises exists, so managing a brand's online reputation is essential.

In conclusion, social media marketing is an indispensable tool in today's marketing landscape. Its reach, affordability, interactivity, and data-driven approach make it a key element in any marketing strategy. When executed effectively, social media marketing can boost brand awareness, drive sales, and foster a strong connection with the target audience. Businesses that embrace social media marketing and adapt to its dynamic nature will have a significant advantage in the modern business environment.

Made in the USA
Las Vegas, NV
11 January 2024